FOR

It is a great privilege for m   s
to you in the name of the C   1
March 1st 1994 we launche
rebuild and restore the Wil........ ....   e
Cathedral since 1834. This is the greatest challenge that has
faced the Cathedral Chapter for the last twenty five years,
and we are indebted to all who help us as we strive to raise
this monumental sum of money.

Personally, I have been greatly encouraged by the
spontaneous offers of help that I have received. This volume
is one such venture. I would like to thank Mr.David Wyke
of St Asaph, who has collected all the material contained in
this book, he has collated it and been wholly responsible for
its publication. The result is proof of his enthusiasm and
drive, and I congratulate him most warmly.

I pray that you will find the contents useful and indeed
entertaining, as Mr Wyke has been able to include the
traditional, the modern and the unusual. It is amazing how
many different ways there are of saying "Thank You" to God
for all His benefits.

Kerry Goulstone
Dean

GRACE

" A short prayer either asking a blessing before or rendering thanks after, a meal."

QED

From the Latin, Gratias, Thanks.

PREFACE

This anthology is a collection of Graces given freely by the many friends of St Asaph Cathedral, Some are very formal, some humorous, some dredged from the deepest recesses of memory, some composed for the occasion; but all have one thing in common, they are thanking God for the gift of food , and with it the gift of life. The saying of Grace or Thanksgiving, is not restricted to Christianity, and we have been most fortunate to have contributions from other faiths and from other countries. We have also be able to include Graces written in the original languages of the British Isles, Welsh, Irish, Gaelic, Manx and Cornish, as well as Middle English and Latin.

My thanks go to the many contributors who have provided such a mixed variety of Graces and to those who have contributed spiritually and materially to this project.

I am indebted to Ray Forkings , who has helped enormously in the preparation of this manuscript, to my wife for undertaking the laborious task of proof-reading, and to all those who have provided numerous helpful suggestions throughout this undertaking.

I am also grateful to the Masters and Fellows of the many colleges who have submitted Graces and the Harp Lager Company Ltd for the permission to publish a number of extracts from the Harp Book of Graces. Finally I must give thanks to the St Asaph Cathedral Organ Restoration Appeal without which I would never have launched into this most stimulating exercise.

David T Wyke

OCTOBER 1994

The Cathedral Organ

The present organ at St. Asaph Cathedral began life in 1834 when William Hill, one of the greatest and most revolutionary organ builders of the age built a small instrument on a specially constructed screen under the western tower arch. During the following twenty-five years, this instrument was enlarged and improved until St. Asaph Cathedral possessed one of the finest and largest Cathedral organs in the country.

The fact that this excellent early Victorian material forms the core of the present instrument makes our Cathedral organ very special. Most other Cathedral organs were substantially reconstructed during the last forty years of the last century, but, apart from some new stops, new mechanism and a move to the north transept, St.Asaph's organ remained very much unchanged. It not only sounded wonderful but it looked impressive too, and contemporary photographs show tall sixteen-foot pipes soaring up to the roof above the pinnacles of the Canons' stalls which were, until 1931, positioned in the crossing beneath the tower.

In 1931, it was realised that the massive central tower was in a perilous state and near to collapse. While essential work was done to the foundations, the organ was dismantled and stored. When the work was completed, the opportunity was taken to re-order that area of the Cathedral and the Canon's stalls were moved eastwards to the presbytery. The organ was re-erected, but with a redesigned facade, greatly cut down in height, which lacked the imposing scale of the previous display pipes. However the sound of the organ remained unchanged until

1966, when the organ was substantially rebuilt. Changes were made which, with the benefit of hindsight and a more sympathetic attitude to early Victorian organ-building, can now be seen to be not in the best interests of the organ. The keyboards were moved from the gallery to the floor level, some pipework was removed and replaced with new material not in keeping with the old nineteenth century pipework and the facade was painted bright blue. This might have been fashionable in the mid-sixties, but know remains an eyesore in this beautiful medieval building.

However, the former glories can be easily restored, but it will cost a lot of money. I feel that the organ must not only sound magnificent but it must be a thing of great visual beauty as well. The proposed case-design, to be executed in carved oak, has exceeded all our expectations. The production of this excellent book will make a significant contribution to our fund-raising efforts as we aim to give St.Asaph Cathedral one of the best organs in this country.

Hugh Davies
September 1994

CHAPTER 1

A Miscellany of Graces

"Let us give Thanks"

"Benedictus Benedicat."

The Rt Hon Sir Edward Heath KG.MBE.MP

**"For What We Are About To Receive,
May The Lord Make Us Truly Thankful"**

Rt Hon Lord Callaghan Of Cardiff KG.

**Father, we thank you for this food and for
those who prepared it; may our eating of it
be a sign of our union one with another and
with your Son, Jesus Christ Our Lord.**

*THE BISHOP OF BRISTOL
The Right Reverend Barry Rogerson*

"In a world where many are hungry let us give thanks for our food:

In a world where many are unemployed let us give thanks for our work:

In a world where many despair let us give thanks for hope in Jesus Christ our Lord".

THE BISHOP OF LIVERPOOL
The Rt Revd David Sheppard

TEMPERANCE SOCIETY DINNER

Lord of Cana, Lord Divine,
Who changed the water into wine.
Look down upon these foolish men
Who seek to change it back again.

A GRACE THE BISHOP USES WHEN HE HIMSELF HAS PREPARED THE MEAL

" Bless this mess ! "

THE BISHOP OF BATH AND WELLS
The Right Reverend James Thompson

GRACE USED BEFORE A MEAL IN THE RECTORY SETTING :

"O Lord, bless this home and those who live here : may your peace rest upon them and all who come to this home be they friend or stranger and make us mindful of your mercy as we enjoy the blessings of this hospitality, through Jesus Christ our Lord.

Amen."

THE ARCHBISHOP OF ARMAGH
The Most Reverend Dr.R.H.A.Eames

For food and drink and friendship we render
thanks, O God,
Deepen Our Gratitude,
Enlarge our sympathies,
And order our affections in generous and
unselfish lives,
Through Jesus Christ our Lord.

FROM THE BISHOP OF OXFORD
The Right Reverend Richard Harries

'Come Lord Jesus be our guest and bless what
thou has given us '

THE ARCHBISHOP OF YORK
The Most Reverend John Habgood

For food, in a world where many walk in hunger
For faith, in a world where many walk in fear,
For friends, in a world where many walk alone
We give you humble thanks, O Lord.

THE BISHOP OF BLACKBURN
The Right Reverend Alan Chesters M.A.

'Lord, thy glory fills the heaven;
 Earth is with its fullness stored;
Unto thee be glory given,
 Holy, Holy, Holy, Lord. '

DEAN OF WINDSOR
The Very Reverend Patrick Mitchell,

"Bless oh Lord our food and our wine,
For Holy You are now and forever,
World without end, Amen".

THE AMBASSADOR GREEK EMBASSY LONDON
Elias Gounaris

Creator of all good things,
M*A*y your blessing
Come dow*N* upon this food & drink
Make our h*A*nds strong to serve you
In both will & *D*eed so that
The whole wide world m*A*y give you glory.

Submitted by THE HIGH COMMISSIONER FOR CANADA
Composed By Canon Of Westminster And Rector Of St.Margaret's

Some have food and cannot eat,
Some would eat and have no food :
We have food and we can eat, let us
thank God.

COLONEL THE LORD LANGFORD, O.B.E. D.L.

Grant, Lord that we may in due proportion and
due time eat well, drink wisely, listen attentively
and speak caringly ; and thereafter journey
comfortably and arrive home safely.

The Lord Rix C.B.E. D.L.

May our stomachs forgive us what we are about to eat, our wits what we are about to drink, and our consciences what we are about to say.

The Lord Rix C.B.E. D.L.

"Dear Lord
Please make this food taste better
than its appearance or smell may suggest it
will taste. Through Jesus Christ our Lord"

Auberon Waugh

For Boiled, Fried, Grilled or Roast
Praise Father, Son and Holy Ghost.

Ronnie Hazlehurst

**"May we who are sinners
Deserve our dinners".**

Rabbi Lionel Blue

**For the tea marmalade and toast
Thank you Lord, and the Holy Ghost**

Anon

**O God, Ruler of the Seven Seas
Bless these chips and fish and peas**

Anon

Bless this bunch as they munch their lunch

Anon

Be present O Lord, at our table tonight

Anon

Traditionally given by parents to their children on the eve of the Sabbath, before the family meal.

"The Eternal bless and preserve thee! The Eternal cause his countenance to shine upon thee, and be gracious unto thee ! The Eternal direct his countenance towards thee, and grant thee peace"
AMBASSADOR OF ISRAEL
Mr Moshe Raviv.

WELSH GUARDS COLLECT

O. LORD GOD. who has given us the Land of our Fathers for our inheritance, help Thy servants, the Welsh Guards, to keep Thy Laws as our heritage for ever, until we come to that better and heavenly country which Thou hast prepared for us : through Jesus Christ our Lord.

R.H.Q. - WELSH GUARDS

This is attributed to the Very Revd. Lancelot Fleming, when Dean of Windsor.

"O Lord grant that we may not be like porridge,
Still, stodgy and hard to stir,
But like cornflakes, crisp, fresh and ready to serve".

This is attributed to Geoffrey Fisher, former Archbishop of Canterbury and quite useful for children's parties !.

"For what we are about to receive and for what some have already snatched, may the Lord make us truly thankful".

THE GROUPED PARISHES OF ST ASAPH and TREMEIRCHION with CEFN
Reverend Robert H Griffiths

Grace for a family meal

We thank you God for all you have given us and especially this meal we now share. May we be grateful for the work of those whose hands have brought our food from field to table. This we ask in Jesus' name
Amen
REVD SHIRLEY T GRIFFITHS

Lord God you have given us so much.
Give us one thing more, give us grateful hearts
and make us ever mindful of the needs of others.

From a nervous cleric
" Make us ever needful of the minds of others"

BISHOP OF BANGOR
Rt Rev. Barry Morgan

Oh Lord who turned the water into wine
Why do you let so many people reverse the
process.

Sir Clement Freud

Our Father, we bow in your presence and give thanks for your provision for our daily needs

We thank you for food, shelter and clothing ; for freedom to worship you, for family and friends.

In a world where thousands are deprived of life's basic necessities, you have blessed us abundantly.

Help us then to recognize that we are "our brother's keeper" and, as a result, reach out to our world with care and compassion.

In the name of Jesus Christ, our Savour and Lord.

GENERAL Bramwell Tillsley
THE SALVATION ARMY

O Lord : in a world where many are lonely :
Make us thankful for our community.

In a world where many are sick :
Bless those who bring healing.

In a world where many are hungry :
Give us a hunger for your love and compassion.

That with thankful and wholesome lives
We may bless your holy name.
                              Amen

                              Terry Waite

We thank the creator of all good things for the food and wine we are about to enjoy ever mindful of those not so fortunate as ourselves. We are truly grateful to those who have grown it, those who have prepared it and those who serve it, But before all we praise and thank the Almighty for his bountiful provision. Amen

LORD FORTE OF RIPLEY

A GRACE FOR USE AT SEA:

Bless this company, bless this meat :
Thank God for galley and for Fleet.

AN AWFUL GRACE AFTER DINNER :

For dishes inside us, and those beside us !
We thank you Lord.

Good wine
Good meet
Good Lord
Replete !

A GRACE FOR DINNER ATTENDED BY A NUMBER OF
SENIOR PEOPLE :

Lord thanks for our leaders
And for the led
For partners and guests
And daily bread

May we who have been so richly fed
In service of others now be led

**Some words of thanks I now must utter
And over more than bread and butter.
Thank God for wives, friends, food and wine
And 'specially for St Valentine**

A GRACE ATTRIBUTED TO ADMIRAL LORD NELSON

**God save the King (Queen)
Bless our victuals
And make us thankful.**

CHAPLAIN OF THE FLEET & ARCHDEACON FOR THE
ROYAL NAVY
The Venerable M W Bucks QHC BD AKC

"Christ God bless the food and drink of thy servants
for Holy art thou always, now and ever and unto
the ages of ages
Amen"

ORTHODOX CHURCH of the HOLY PROTECTION
T he Russian Orthodox Church in Wales, Blaenau Ffestiniog
The Very Reverend Father Deiniel

"Be present at our table Lord
Be here and everywhere ador'd.
These creatures bless and grant that we
May feast in paradise with Thee. "

"Thanks to God for good food and friends
and family to share it with. Pray for those who lack
such simple happiness."

Joe Wilson
MEMBER OF THE EUROPEAN PARLIAMENT FOR
NORTH   WALES

The Airborne Forces Grace

**"Good food; Good Friends'. Safe Landings ;
Thank God".**

REGIMENTAL HEADQUARTERS THE 22ND(CHESHIRE)REGIMENT
THE CASTLE CHESTER

A GRACE FROM THE LOWLANDS OF SCOTLAND

**Doon wi' yer heed
Up wi' yer paws
An' thank the laird
For the use o' yer jaws**
Thelma Barlow
Coronation Street

The Revd. Sidney Smith used to say Graces as follows;
If he observed the table laid with but one set of knifes and forks and one glass he would say " For these the least of these thy mercies we give thee humble thanks " ; but if he saw a generous array of cutlery and three or four wine glasses for each place setting he would begin " O bounteous Jehovah, who has poured forth thy blessings upon us..............."

Sir Antony Meyer

THE GRACE FROM KEELE UNIVERSITY

" May Grace be given to us to thanke God for All".

THE PRINCESS MARGARET, COUNTESS OF SNOWDON.
Former Chancellor, Keele University

Bless, O Lord, this food to our use,
This occasion to our enjoyment,
And ourselves in your service :
And make us generous in the help we give
to those in need
Through Jesus Christ our Lord

THE BISHOP OF HEREFORD
The Rt.Revd.John Oliver

**"We thank you Lord for meat and beans,
But most of all for Royal Marines".**

THE LORD BISHOP OF SODOR & MAN
The Rt. Revd. Noel Jones

**For food in a land where people walk in hunger.
For faith in a land where people walk in dread.
And for our friends and our families, in a land
where people walk alone.
For these Blessings, we give Thee our thanks.
Amen**

**For what we are about to receive
May the Lord grant us tolerance and a true
understanding.   Amen**

MEMBER OF PARLIAMENT FOR DELYN
David Hanson MP

Send down, O Lord
Plenteous blessings on us and on all we
Eat and drink this day ;
And may we always
Keep in mind
Everyone who tonight will go to
Rest hungry or thirsty.

MADAM SPEAKER
Betty Boothroyd MP

"Bless us as we meet around your table, and
grant that in our life we may reflect your
wisdom and your compassion"

THE RIGHT HONOURABLE VISCOUNT TONYPANDY PC, DC

"Lord, we ask you to bless us and our friendship as we sit down to this meal. Bless all those who have helped toprovide and prepare these good things for us and help us to bear in mind the needs of those in whose lives there are no such good things.
We ask this through Christ our Lord.
AMEN "

THANKS AFTER A MEAL

"Father, we give you thanks for this meal and all it has meant to us. We ask you to bless in this life or in eternal life all those who have eaten here before us. Through Christ our Lord.   AMEN."

THE SUPERIOR, ST BEUNO'S LLANELWY,
M.K.O'Halloran, S.J.

For food in a world where many walk hungry;
For faith in a world where many walk in fear ;
For fellowship in a world where many walk alone ;
We give you humble thanks, O Lord. Amen.

OCCASIONALLY USED IN THE ROYAL NAVY

O Lord, who blessed the loaves and fishes,
We give you thanks for these our dishes ;
And ever may our souls be fed
By you, O Christ, the Living Bread. Amen

BISHOP OF ST DAVIDS
The Right Reverend J.Ivor Rees

THIS IS ANONYMOUSLY ATTRIBUTED TO A
DURHAM MINER ABOUT 1800

"What we're about the receive has nowt to do wi' the
Duke of Newcastle."

MEMBER OF PARLIAMENT FOR CLWYD SOUTH WEST
Martyn Jones, MP.

God of Goodness, bless our food
Keep us in a pleasant mood,
Bless the cooks and all who serve us,
From indigestion Lord preserve us,
And if long speeches we endure
Give us first a good liqueur.
                              Amen

May the meal that we share
Be seasoned from above with
Thy blessings and thy grace,
But most of all, Thy love,
For Jesus' sake.
                              Amen

THE BISHOP OF SWANSEA AND BRECON
The Rt.Revd.Dewi M.Bridges, M.A.

TWO GRACES BEFORE AND AFTER DINNER
AT THE MIDDLE TEMPLE

GRACE BEFORE MEAT

THE eyes of all things look up and put their trust in Thee, O Lord! Thou givest them their Meat in due season ; Thou openest thine hands, and fillest with Thy blessing every living thing. Good Lord bless us and these Thy good gifts which we receive, of Thy bounteous liberality, through Jesus Christ our Lord. Amen

GRACE AFTER MEAT.

GLORY, honour, and praise be given to Thee, O Lord, who dost feed us from our tender age, and givest sustenance to every living thing. Replenish our hearts with joy and gladness, that we, having sufficient, may be rich and plentiful in all good works, through Jesus Christ our Lord. God save his Church, the Queen, all the Royal Family, and this Realm ; God send us peace and truth in Christ our Lord. Amen

THE RT.HON. THE LORD HOWE OF ABERAVON. QC

COMPOSED FOR THE MAUNDY LUNCH 1994

Our grateful worship Lord we pay
on this thy humble Maundy Day.
And grant that as thy servants dine
on bounteous gifts of food and wine,
Our thanks would raise to thee above
for all these benefits of love
And also joy and homage show
to those who reign for thee below

Amen

**For horse hair wig and woolsack seat,
Praise Father, Son and Paraclete.
For rights preserved and justice done,
Praise Father, Holy Ghost and Son.
For Judges, Clerks and PCs Plod,
Praise Son and Holy Ghost and God.
Amen**

THE BISHOP OF TRURO
Rt Revd Micheal Thomas

The place was deepest Africa. The occasion was a multi-racial dinner party. My host was suddenly called upon to say grace. He told me afterwards that the words in the African vernacular momentarily deserted him. What he actually said was-

"Ichabod camouflage hip bath hip bath. Amen".

What I have to tell you is that the "Amen" was thunderously pronounced, and the meal was excellent.

THE REVD. THE LORD SOPER.

"As Chancellor of Oxford I am surprisingly rarely called upon to pronounce a Grace : many speeches, some in Latin, some in English, but few Graces. This is because I am mostly able to call upon a distinguished diocesan to perform this function. Oxford is often available, but on one occasion when he was not, I was able to persuade Winchester, Cantabrigian but Visitor like me of no less than five Oxford colleges, to perform this function at a notable dinner for the opening of the Bodleian fund-raising campaign in 1989 when we dined with the Prince of Wales in the Radcliffe Camera, in which a dinner had not been held since the Emperor of Russia, the King of Prussia and the Prince Regent had dined there in a somewhat premature celebration of the downfall of Napoleon in 1814.

The CHANCELLOR OF THE UNIVERSITY OF OXFORD
The Rt. Hon. Lord Jenkins of Hillhead O.M.

Thank God for food and raiment
and a soft pillow for your head
May you be forty years in heaven
before the Devil knows you are dead.

Lord, who blessed the bread and wine
We ask your blessing as we dine
If there are speeches to endure
Pray God we're served a good liquer.
General Sir John Mogg
GCB, CBE, DSO, DL.

In a world where many are lonely;
  we thank you for friendship and community:
In a world where many are despairing ;
  we thank you for hope:
In a world which many find meaningless, ;
  we thank you for faith :
In a world where many are hungry;
  we thank you for this food.
Through Christ, our Lord Amen

PERSONAL GRACE SAID AT DINNERS, WEDDINGS
BREAKFASTS ETC.

O God our heavenly father, the giver of all good things, we give you thanks for all your many blessings to us, especially for this food and this fellowship. Amen

Assistant Bishop, In St.Asaph
Rt.Revd.Huw Jones,

Bless all who gather in this room;
and bless Good Lord what we consume.
                                    Amen
       We thank thee, Lord
       for bed and board.
                 Amen
For gravy, veg and Sunday roast
Bless Father Son and Holy Ghost
                                    Amen

        Almighty God, we thank you
        for physical food
        and spiritual nurture
        in and through the love
        of Jesus Christ, your son.
                                    Amen
      We thank you Lord,
        O hear us pray,
For food that we've been eating,
and when its freezing like today
Thanks too for central heating. Amen
                              Frank Topping

Thou hast given so much to us
Grant one thing more. Thankful hearts
Thro Jesus Christ our Lord.

May we not be thankful when it pleases us,
As tho the choice was ours,
But grant such hearts to pulse with thanks
for all eternity.

If the only prayer we say,
Each day of life,
Be "Thank You" then it will suffice.   Amen

In everything give thanks : for this is the will of God
In Christ Jesus concerning us all.
(I Thess.5.18)

We rejoice and give thanks for Earthworms/Bees/Lady
Birds/and Hens
For the rising of the sap,
The fragrance of growth
for the tending of our gardens..
We celebrate and give thanks.   Amen

Grant us thankful hearts O God for all your
Goodness and when help us to live so that our
Thankfulness be daily reflected. Thro Jesus Christ
Our Lord.
O God of love make us more thankful for all the
boundless. Mercies of daily life. Filling our lives
with gratitude and our lips with praise. Amen

For the blessings of home and family life,
for all the gifts of friendship,
for all that enriches our lives.
make us ever more worthy of your bounty, Amen

Heavenly Father you have graciously given us
he resources of this world : May we gratefully
receive and accept them to your Glory

Grant that we and all our fellow men may enjoy
the blessings of a just society and live together
freely sharing to meet all our mutual needs.

Lord hasten the day when no human being shall
live in contentment whilst knowing that others are
in need. Amen

Collected by The Revd J.Parry
Abbeyfield House Rhyl
Contributed By Councillor Trevor Roberts, Former Mayor of St Asaph

FOR THOSE WHO WANT TO SAY.A TABLE GRACE

PRESENTED WITH THE MEAL - CONTINENTAL
AIRWAYS U.S.A.

ROMAN CATHOLIC

**"Bless us, O Lord, and these thy gifts, which
we are about receive from thy bounty. Through
Christ our Lord Amen"**

JEWISH

**"Lift up your hands toward the sanctuary and bless
the Lord. Blessed art thou, O Lord our God, King
of the universe, who bringest forth bread from the
earth."**

PROTESTANT

**"Bless, O Lord, this food to our use, and us to Thy
service, and make us ever mindful of the needs of
others, in Jesus' name. Amen"**

Mr Churchman

"For food and all who prepared it,
For health & fellowship and all who share it,
And mindful always of all who need it
We thank thee, Lord our God; Amen"

Dean Raymond Renowden

It is alleged that a Dean of Winchester was invited to a prestigious luncheon on a yacht during Cowes Week, He was asked to say Grace, Just as he was about to begin, an unexpected squall hit the yacht and it keeled over, He said,

"For what we are likely to retain,
may the Lord make us truly thankful,
Amen"

Dean Raymond Renowden

" When I first started teaching in a school in Lancashire, the saying of Grace was the responsibility of the member of staff in charge of the school lunch. On my first day, I nervously called the assembly to order with, "Eyes together, hands closed". Needless to say the kids   responded with enthusiasm!"

Colin Welland

Lord be blessed for the light of this day
Be blessed for those gathered around this table

Lord be blessed for the food you give us
Blessed be your name, Father, Son and Holy Ghost

Antonius Jan Glazemaker
Archbishop of Utrecht
Old Catholic Church / Union of Utrecht

Knows the ox his master's stable,
And shall we
Not know thee,
Nourished at thy table ?
Yes, of all good gifts the giver
Thee we own,
Thee alone
Magnify for ever.

SAID IN TOO MUCH OF A HURRY:

" Lord, make us needful of the minds of others"

Father in heaven,
loving and good
bless Christmas Dinner
and the Christmas Pud
Amen

BEFORE CORNFLAKES :

"Lord, make us crisp and always ready to serve"

"For every cup and plateful God make us truly grateful"

AT A WEDDING

For the happiness of this special day
For the pleasure of each others company
For the food we are about to enjoy
and for the love which supplies all our needs
God's holy name be praised
Amen

Superintendent Minister
Rev. James C. Poore, BD.,
THE METHODIST CHURCH
BEVERLEY CIRCUIT

**" Come, Lord Jesus, be our Guest
May this food to us be bless'd"**

THE ARCHBISHOP OF CANTERBURY
Most Reverend George Carey

A GRACE SUITABLE FOR A GOLF DINNER

**O Thou, who in thy heaven above
Sits smiling as we swing,
For giving us the game we love
Accept the praise we bring.**

**Now sit and join us, Lord of all
And fill us with Thy grace,
Whilst those who smite the wee white ball
Make glad within this place.**

THE EDINBURGH ACADEMY
Chaplain, Rev. Howard J.Haslett

"We thank Thee, Lord, for daily bread
As by Thy hands our souls are fed.
Grant us to grow more like to Thee
Today and through eternity".

Professor Eric Sunderland
Principal University of Wales
BANGOR

Bless our fellowship
Bless our fun
And Bless the work
the cooks have done
Amen

Evelyn Glennie OBE

"Blessed art thou O Lord our God, King of the
Universe,who bringest forth bread from the earth.
Amen

The Revd. Dr.P.J.Jagger. Warden and Chief Librarian
SAINT DEINIOL'S LIBRARY
HAWARDEN

A prayer for you is said to-day
May the love of God ever with you stay
Please bless this food wherever we are
May the blessing of God ever rest on you

God bless this food
And bless those who have prepared it
And make us always mindful
of those in need who have nothing to eat.

TRANSLATIONS FROM ARABIC
Thank you God for feeding me and watering me.

O, God, give me strength, for I am weak
Give me pride for I am humble
Give me wealth for I am impoverished
O God the most merciful.

O God, I ask you for the company of fearfulness
The triumph of longing
The constancy of science
The continuity of intellect
O God, the most merciful

O God, I take refuge in you
Against worry and grief
Against impotence and sloth,
O God, I take refuge in you from need
Except to you,
From humility,
Except to you,
From fear
Except from you,
Oh God the most merciful.

EMBASSY OF THE UNITED ARAB EMIRATES
Easa Saleh Al-Gurg, CBE.,
Ambassador

**Come, Lord Jesus, be our guest;
And let thy gifts to us be blessed**

BISHOP OF MONMOUTH
Rt Revd Rowan Williams

**"May He who blessed the loaves and fishes,
'Bless the Mothers' Union and these dishes'.**

Mrs Harris, Central President of the Mothers' Union,

THE BOWLER'S PRAYER

**Lord grant that when my woods I bowl
Whate'er the length may be,
Not merry or how short they roll
But on the jack score two for me.**

Jack Stone - ST ASAPH BOWLS CLUB

THE DINNER PARTY GRACE

For the safety of arrival
For the gaiety of welcome
For the closeness of family,
-the companionship of friends;

For the pleasure of food,
-the benison of wine,
For the fondness of talk,
-the comfort of digestion

For the pang of parting
-the last guest leaving.
For these we give thanks.
And for those who have none
of these things,
We seek your special blessing.

Joan Bakewell

O Lord
Bless those who *have not* what I have
Convert those who *care not* that others need
Increase your love that we *hurt not* our neighbour
Feed us both food and spirit that we *fail not*
To eat with gladness and serve with joy.
                                                    Amen

The Rev.Edgar G.Adams, Rector ST ASAPH 'S CHURCH
           BALA CYNWYND, PENNSYLVANIA, USA

Lord bless us and these thy
gifts which of thy mercy we
receive, for Christs sake. Amen

                        Stuart Smith
                   ASSISTANT BISHOP
              ADELAIDE, SOUTH AUSTRALIA

One word is as good as ten, Dig in, Amen

Anon
Australia

For family, friends and good food God's Holy name be praised

THE DEAN OF ST ASAPH
The Very Reverend Kerry Gouldstone

Lord, bless our fellowship, bless our food and make us mindful of the needs of others.

The Most Revd Alwyn Rice Jones
ARCHBISHOP OF WALES

**Gracious God - Creator and Father,
For this food and for every gift of Your love,
We give heartfelt thanks
in the Name of Jesus Christ Our Lord. Amen**

THE BISHOP OF CHESTER
The Rt.Revd.Michael A.Baughen

**We thank you Lord for all our food
On every day that passeth,
And for our Bishops and the Clergy
Especially in St Asaph.**

John & Anne Prys Williams

May the good Lord give our jaws the power
To crush what we've about to devour.

David Blott

A GRACE FOR A WEDDING

For food and drink and celebration,
For holy times and relaxation
For marriage, family and friends-
Praise God whose mercy never ends.

The Reverend Canon David Hugh Rees
The Vicarage Meliden

LIAM'S GRACE !

Oh God of the held-out spoon
With the puréed carrot and prune.
I thank you that when I sat and cried,
am's blest response was - ' Open wide' !

Yvonne Davies
St Asaph Library

FROM AN OLD ROSSENDALE LADY

"Sit thi down an rest thi feet
An thank the Lord fer summat to eat"

" Fer food an friendship at this table
'Lets' give HIM thanks whilst we art able".

AN OLD MAN FROM DARWEN

"Fer food that's gradely an served wi lov
Let's thank YON MON in heaven above

HEARD AT A SUNDAY SCHOOL TEA-PARTY

"We thank thee Lord fer what wir gettin
If thir'd bin moar on't plate
Moar would a bin etten."

FROM A LANCASHIRE SCHOOL, FOR SCHOOL DINNERS.

"For what we are about to receive-
May the Lord give us strength ter eat it!"

FROM A CHAPEL IN ROSSENDALE

"For food we eat, and those who prepare it.
For health to enjoy it and friends to share it ;
We thank thee O Lord, Amen

Contributed By BENITA L. MOORE

GRACE AT A WEDDING BREAKFAST

Thank you for the love that brought us here.
Thank you for the food to give us cheer.
Thank you Lord that on you we can call.
Thank the brides father, he's paying for it all.

A SHORT GRACE

At a Navy mess dinner, the Captain was asked
much to his surprise to say Grace , He stood up
and said "Is the parde here ?"
'No', was the quick reply.
'Thank God' said the Captain and sat down.

REV C A & MRS SPARKES
Hawkinge
Kent

A RUGBY GRACE
Lord. thank you for opportunity ;
The opportunity of rugby football
It's opportunities in playing,
  in refereeing, in coaching,
  in organising, in supporting,

It's opportunities in fellowship
  and friendship;
And especially tonight in this dinner.

Lord, give us justification for
  anticipating a good night.

Bless this food and drink we are
about to receive to our use,
  And ourselves to your use and purpose
            Amen

ADAM ROBSON
PRESIDENT
SCOTTISH RUGBY UNION
1983/84

For this food, fellowship and the chance
To serve St Asaph
We thank you

Lord bless this bunch as they munch their lunch,
make them ever mindful of the needs of this
cathedral and May they dig deep in their pockets to
restore this big piano.

Ron Kitchin
Pittendreich

CURLERS' GRACE

O Lord, Wha's Love surrounds us a',
An' brings us a' th'gither,'
Wha' writes your Laws upon our hearts,
and bids us help each ither.

We bless Thee for Thy Bounties great,
For meat and hame and gear,
We thank Thee, Lord, for snaw and ice,
But still we'd ask for mair.

Gie' us a hert to dae whits richt,
Like Curlers true and keen,
To be guid friends alang life's road,
And soop our slide aye clean.

NB Usually spoken by the club Captain
The Royal Caledonian Curling Club
M.G.THOMPSON
Secretary

A FOOTBALL GRACE
For soup and meat and fresh ice cream
And for our famous football team
Amen

Rev Nigel Sands
Chaplain CRYSTAL PALACE F.C.

POTATO GRACE

Bless the potato and the land where it grew,
Bless those who planted it, and those who eat it,
Especially the people of Uist and Harris;
But you can do what you like with the people of
Lewis. Amen
Translated from the Gaelic by Rev Norman McDonald
Perth Scotland

With grateful heart we acknowledge the giver-
And all who have laboured that we can eat.
Lord, may the day be near when people everywhere
Will partake of your Bounty and rejoice in the
Love of Christ. Amen

Rev John Kitchin
ST.ANDREWS, SCOTLAND

Morning (Evening) is here
The board is spread
Thanks be to God
Who gives us bread

Gill Winter

A FARMERS GRACE

Let the wealthy and great
Roll in splendour and state
I envy them not I declare it;
I eat my own lamb
My chickens and ham
I shear my own fleece and I wear it.
I have lawns I have bowers
I have fruit, I' have flowers
The lark my morning alarmer
So my jolly boys now
Here'i God speed the plough
Long life and success to the farmer.

Sylvia Harris

GRACE BEFORE MEALS

Bless us, O Lord, and these your gifts which we are about to receive from your bounty. Through Christ our Lord. Amen

GRACE AFTER MEALS

We give you thanks, Almighty God, for all your benefits, who live and reign, for ever and ever. May the souls of the faithful departed, through the mercy of God, rest in peace. Amen

Mr.Joseph Begley
Penyffordd.

' Father, help us to see you illuminate the most mundane things of daily round, and most of all, help us to experience the life-changing force of Christ in us. Holy Spirit bless this time together of refreshments and nourishment. !

Gerald Williams

Here a little child I stand
Heaving up my either hand
Cold as puddocks though they be,
Here I lift them up to thee,
For a benison to fall,
on our meat and on us all

(Puddocks are toads)

Rt.Hon Lord Healey of Riddlesden CH MBE.

THE POOR EAT and are satisfied ; those who seek the Lord shall praise Him, and their heart shall live for ever and ever.

THEN THE ARCHBISHOP BLESSES THE TABLE
O Christ God, bless the food and drink of your servants, for You are Holy, now and always and for ever and ever. R Amen Lord have mercy, Lord have mercy, Lord have mercy

THEN THE DEACON GOES TO THE ARCHBISHOP BOWS TO HIM AND TO ALL THE BRETHREN AND SAYS
Give me your blessing, holy brethren, and forgive me a sinner.
R. May the Lord forgive you and have mercy on you.

THEN THE DEACON TAKES THE PANAGIA WITH HIS FINGERS. ELEVATES IT SLIGHTLY, AND SAYS ALOUD
Great is the name.
R. Of the Holy Trinity

**O most holy Mother of God, help us.
R Through her prayers, O God, have mercy on us
and save us.**

**ALL-PURE LADY who gave birth to God, your
womb has become a holy table, bearing the
heavenly Bread, Christ our God : he who eats of
Him shall not die, according to the promise of the
Creator of all and our Provider.**

R. Make us worthy of your gifts, O Virgin Mother of God :
forget our transgressions and be attentive to the voice of those
who receive your blessing in faith, O Immaculate One.

**IT IS FITTING and right to call you blessed, O
Theotokos, the ever-blessed and blameless one and
the Mother of our God. O you higher in honour
than the Cherubim and more glorious beyond
compare than the Seraphim, you gave birth to God
the Word in virginity. You are truly Mother of
God ; you do we exalt.**

You have gladdened our hearts, O Lord, in the
things You created for us. We have been made
secure through the works of your hands. Let the
light of your countenance shine upon us, O Lord.
You have gladdened my heart. In peace I will
sleep, and I will repose in You, for You, O Lord,
have sustained my hope beyond measure.
-Glory be to the Father and to the Son and to the
Holy Spirit, now and always and for ever and ever.
Amen
-Lord, have mercy (Three Times)
-Give the blessing, Father.

AND <u>THE</u> <u>ARCHBISHOP</u> <u>SAYS</u> :

May God be with us in his grace and in his love for
mankind, at all times, now always and for ever and
ever.
R. Amen

And they begin the (evening) meal.

ARCHBISHOP GREGORIOS OF THYATEIRA AND
GREAT BRITAIN

O Lord and giver of all good
We praise thee for our daily food
May St Asaph friends and St Asaph ways
Help us to serve thee all our days.

Some live to eat, some eat to live
Some people take, some people give,
Lord grant that we, who eat three meals a day
Should sometimes stop to think and say
That whilst we thank thee for this daily food
Remember those who would eat, if they could

Main course - sweet and coffee too
And we'll clear the lot as we always do
But if we had to go without for days on end
We'd know what it was to be like those
Who think not of _what_ to eat - but _when_

We love to eat, we like to drink
And worry little of the price
But help us Lord to remember those
Who would give thanks, for just a bowl of rice

Some hae' meat and canna eat
Some hae' nae' meat and want it.
But we hae' meat and we can eat.
And so the Lord be thank it

Before we raise our knife and forks
And listen to popping corks
Help us Lord to think and pray
For those who will not eat today

Lord, make us not like porridge
Stodgy and hard to stir
But make us more like cornflakes
Crisp and ready to serve.

THE SCOTTISH TRANSLATION

O Lord grant that we may not be like Cornflakes -
Lightweight - Brittle and cold,
But like Porridge - Warm, Comforting and full of
Natural Goodness.

We come to the table - Hungry and dry
And to satisfy that we are willing to try
That we are the lucky ones no one will deny
Lets remember those who if they don't eat - may
die

Ron Kitchin

MASONIC

For what we are about to receive may the Great Architect of the Universe make truly grateful and ever watchful and mindful of the wants and needs of others. So mote it be

Anon

May he who blessed the loaves and fishes, bless also these poor little dishes. They may indeed be very small, but please the Lord they'll feed us all.

Father Patrick O'Donnell
Clonard Monastery Belfast

THE ROUND TABLE GRACE

May we O Lord adopt thy creed
Adapt our ways to serve thy need
And we who on thy bounty feed
Improve in thought, in word and deed

Richard Wynn
MOLD

CHAPTER 2

Graces in Many Languages
"Byddwn ddiolchgar"

CORNISH

GRASSYANS KENS ES DYBRY BOS
(Grace before eating food)

Agan Arluth, ny a'th pys
Gwra benyga agan prys;
Gordhys re by;
Son an bos-ma dh'agan les
Ha ro dhyn bos servons dhys
Bys vynary.

Our Lord, we pray thee,
Hallow our feast;
Be thou worshipped!
Bless this food to our benefit
And give us to be thy servants
For ever.

<u>NS</u> <u>WOSA</u> <u>DYBRY</u> (Grace after eating)

Dhys, Arluth, y-wodhon gras a'gan bos,
Ha bewnans ha yeghes, pup les ty a'n ros;
Dew roy dh 'agan enevow y vanna Ef,
Re bo bara a vewnans danvenys a nef

Thee, Lord, we thank for our food,
And for life and health, and every benefit
which thou hast given us;
May God give his manna to our souls,
May it be the bread of life sent from heaven.

Canon Michael Fisher
St Anta & All Saints Carbis Bay With St Uny Lelant

MIDDLE ENGLISH From The English Register of Godstow Nunnery, near Oxford.

Afore mete, and aftir, gracias say we
Thankyng the, Lorde ! of al thi grete grace;
And for al thi yiftes blessid mote thou be,
Of mete, of drynke, and other solace:
At al due tymes, and in euery place,
Thyne almes is redy to riche and pore:
Euer blessid thou be, good Lorde therfore.

*[Before and after food we offer thanks, thanking you Lord
for all your great grace; and may you be blessed for all your
gifts of food, of drink and of other pleasure; your generosity
is prepared for rich and for poor at all suitable times and in
every place. Thanks be to you good Lord for this always.]*

LADY MARGARET HALL
OXFORD

From Mittelenglische Dichtungen aus der Handschrift 432 des Trinity College in Dublin.

Besechyn benygnely euery creature
That present ben and affterward shal :
Accept soche as ye fynd, to your plesure
Frely offerd with hert, wylle and all

In worship of Kateryne this mayden fre,
Paciently that ye haue it in mynde -
Of what worship ye be or what degre -
To be content with soche as ye fynde,

For norture wol and also ientylnesse,
The diate not replete on a pore borde.
In worship of Mary of hevyn the emperesse
Menske ye the fest with wille, hert and worde.

For myrthe honestly vsed gladeth the company,
Content with litel and mesurably replet.
Wherfore beth mery, I pray you hertly.
And blesse you all this mayde Margaret.

[May it fairly please everyone who is present and who shall come to accept such things as you find, willingly offered for your pleasure with heart, will and everything in honour of this maiden, the noble Katherine, (asking) that you incline yourselves, whatever rank or standing you have, out of your upbringing and your gentleness, to be satisfied with what you find-a meal not abundantly supplied at a poor table. Respect the feast in your will, heart and speech in honour of Mary, empress of heaven. For mirth honourably enjoyed gives pleasure in a company content with little and satisfied with moderation. Therefore be cheerful, I urge you with my heart, and all bless this maiden Margaret.]

LADY MARGARET HALL ,OXFORD

"Byddwn ddiolchgar"
Let us be grateful

Dafydd Wigley M.P.
(Caernarfon)
Brevity is not only the soul of wit, but also helps avoid the food getting cold!- D.W.

BEFORE MEALS

Prions Dgieu-Pour chein qué j'allons r'chéver qué Dgieu s'sait bénit. Amen

Let us pray. For what we are going to receive may God be blessed. Amen.

Prions Dgieu-Au nom du Péthe et du Fis et du Saint Esprit - mangeons, b'vons et èrconnaissons qué tout veint de Dgieu, par Jésû-Christ not' Seigneu. Amen

Let us pray. In the name of the Father and of the Son and of the Holy Spirit - let us eat, let us drink and recognise that everything comes from God, through Jesus Christ our Lord. Amen

AFTER MEALS

**Prions Dgieu - Pour chein qué j'avons r'chu qué
Dgieu s'sait bénit. Amen**

Let us pray. For what we have received may God be blessed. Amen

The Parish Church of St.Ouen with St.George
Brian Vibert,B.A.,St Oeun Jersey

XHOSA SUNG GRACE

Okukutya sikutyayo   *This food we eat*
sikuphiwa nguwe   *we have been given by you,*
nalamanzi siwaselayo   *and this water which we drink*
siwaphiwa nguwe.   *also comes from you.*
Amen   *Amen*

THE ANGLICAN ARCHBISHOP OF CAPE TOWN
The Most Reverend Desmond M Tutu,D.D. F.K.C.

O dad, yn deulu dedwydd-y deuwn.
A diolch o'r newydd,
Can's o'th law y daw bob dydd
Ein lluniaeth a'n llawenydd

O father, a contented family,we come
With renewed thankfulness,
Because from thy hand there comes each day.
Our sustenance and our happiness

Is Popular Grace Has Been Contribuated By Nerys Hughes,
Meurig Rees, Rod Richards MP, And The Rt Revd. Huw Jones

A SWISS PRAYER (IN A HURRY)

Für Trocken und Nasz
Deo Gratias

For dry and wet
Thank God

FOR CHILDREN:

Heer heb dank
voor spijs en drank
voor alle goed
dat Gij ons doet
Amen

> Antonius Jan Glazemaker
> Archbishop of Utrecht
> Old Catholic Church / Union of Utrecht

ALLE VENDER AUGO SINE

Alle vender augo sine til deg
og du gjei dei alli dei a fode i
retti tid.
Du opnar de milde hand, Gud
og mettar alt levande
med hugnad.

All creatures turn their eyes towards You
and You give them all their victuals convenient
You open your gentle hand O God
Pleasantly satisfying all the living creatures

Pastor Tor Grindland
Stavanger Cathedral
Norway

GRACE USED BEFORE A MEAL

"Niño Jesús que naciste en Belén bendice estos alimentos y a nosotros tambien".

Baby Jesus who was born in Bethehem, bless our food and ourselves also

THANKSGIVING PRAYER

"Te damos gracias omnipotente Dios por todo tus beneficios que vives y reinas por los siglo de los siglos, Amén".

We thank you O'God for all your gifts, May you live and reign forever   Amen

EMBAJADA DE ESPAÑA
Dr.Dámaso de Lario
Cultural Counsellor

Poblogoslaw Boze nas i te dary , które z Twojej szczodrobliwosci spozywac mamy. Przez Chrystusa Pana naszego. Amen.

O God! Bless us and those gifts of which we partake thanks to your generosity. Through Jesus Christ our Lord Amen

Dziekujemy Ci wszechmogacy Boze,za wszystkie dobrodziejstwa Twoje,który zyjesz i królujesz na wiekiwieków. Amen.

We are grateful to you O Almighty Lord for all your goodness, You who live and reign for ever and ever Amen

EMBASSY of the REPUBLIC of POLAND
Dr Tadeusz Szumowski
Chargé d'Affaires

Arglwydd,   bendithia ein cymdeithas,
bendithia ein lluniaeth i'n
cadw'n fyw i'th wasanaethu di;

a gwna ni'n ymwybodol o
anghenion pobl eraill yn ein
byd heddiw.

ALWYN ARCHESGOB CYMRU

GRACES IN THE MANX LANGUAGE
OLTAGH ROILSH BEE.

O Hiarn, ta shin guee ort leih dooin ooilley nyn
Beccaghyn,   as cur dty Vannaght orrinyn as
orroo shoh dty Chretooryn mie son yn ymmyd ain:
As cooin lhien dy chur graih dhyt as dy hirveish
oo, yn Fer-toyrt dy chooilley Vie, er Graih Yeesey
Creest. Amen

O Lord, we beseech thee forgive us all our Sins, and Bless us and these thy good Creatures for our use: And assist us to love and serve thee, the Giver of all Good, for Jesus Christ's Sake.

OLTAGH LURG BEE.

O Hiarn, cur orrin ve dy firrinagh booisal son oc shoh as son ooilley dy Vyghinyn elley : As myr ta shin er nyn meaghey liorish dty Aigney, cooin lhien dy veaghey gys dty Ooashley as dty Ghloyr, er Graih Yeesey Creest. Amen

GRACE AFTER MEAT

O. Lord, make us truly thankful for these and all thine other Mercies : And as we are fed by thy Will, assist us to live to thine Honour and Glory, for Jesus Christ's Sake.

OLTAGHEY ROISH IHONGEY

Hiarn bannee ad shoh dty chretooryn mie gys yn ymmyd ain, as shinyn gys dty hirveish, trooid Jeesey Creest nyn Jiarn. Amen

GRACE BEFORE A MEAL

Lord bless these thy good creatures to our use, and us to thy service, through Jesus Christ our Lord.

OLTAGHEY LURG IHONGEY.

Son oc shoh as ooilley e vyghinyn elley, dy row ennym casherick Yee er ny vannaghey as er ny voylley, trooid Yeesey Creest nyn Jiarn. Amen.

GRACE AFTER A MEAL

For these and all his other mercies, the holy name of God be blessed and praised, through Jesus Christ our Lord.

Robert L.Thompson
Isle of Man

SCANDINAVIAN GRACES

<u>SWEDEN</u>   **Gode Gud, välsigna maten, Amen**
Dear God, Bless our food

<u>NORWAY</u>   **Signe maten, Amen**
Bless our food

<u>DENMARK</u>   **Takk gode Gud for alle gaver.**
Thank you dear God for all your gifts.
Velsign maden.
Bless our food.

<u>FINLAND</u>   **Herra, Siunaa ruokamme. Aamen.**
Lord bless our food.
**Siunaa Jeesus ruokamme, ole aina luonamme,
Aamen.**
Bless our food, dear Jesus.
(Mainly used for small chidren)

<u>ICELAND</u>   **God Gud, Blessadu thennan mat sem
vid aetlum   ad borda.**
*Dear God, Bless this food which we are about to
have*

Monica Kielland
BRITISH EMBASSY STOCKHOLM

Bòrd gu'n amhluinn, caithrichean gu'n
chàirdean, dorchadas gu'n briseadh na faire,
saoghal gu'n Slanuighear ! - dubh as an smuain !
Moladh dhuit a h-uile uair a bhriseas sinn aran
aig bòrd ann an co-chomunn chàirdean, gu bheil
Thu a'toirt fo ar comhair neach is e càraid
chis-mhaor agus pheacach, neach is e aran na
beatha, solus a thug buaidh air an dorchadas.
Cuir ar cridhe air ghleus le taingealachd chum
gu'm bi ar beatha na òran molaidh a chuireas cliu
air Dia, is a bheir soillseachadh is misneachd do ar
co-chreutair. Trìd Iosa Criosd ar Tighearna. Amen

*A table without food, chairs without friends, darkness
without a dawn, a world without a redeemer ! - perish the
thought !*
*Praise be that every day we break bread at a table of
fellowship with friends, we are reminded of One who is the
friend of publicans and sinners, of One who is the bread of life,
and of a light that has triumphed over darkness.*
*Attune our heart to thanksgiving so that our life may
become a song of praise, glorifying God, and bringing
inspiration and encouragement into the lives of others. Through
Jesus Christ our Lord. Amen*

Rev, Norman MacDonald
Perth Scotland

The following graces, in French and Breton, have been
collected by Michel Lagadou, Chairman of the Twinning
Association of St Asaphs' twin town of Begard, Brittany

FRENCH

Bénissez nous Seigneur, Bénissez ce repas
Céux qui l'ont préparé,
El procurez du pain à ceux n én
ont pas - Ainsi soit-il.

God bless us, bless this meal,
Those who made it,
And give bread to those who do not have some
So be it. Amen.

Tu es béni, Dies de l'univers
Toi qui nous donnes cepain,
Fruit de la terre et du travail
Des hommes.
Nous te le présentons
Il deviendra le pain de la vie.

Tu es béni, Dieu de l'univers
Toi qui nous donnes ee vin,
Fruit de la vigne et du travail des hommes
Nous te le présentons ;
Il deviendra le vin du royaume éternel

Réponse : Bé soit Dieu, maintenant Et toujours

You are blessed, God of the universe
You, who give this bread
Fruit of the ground and the work of men.
We present it to you
It will become the bread of life.

You are blessed, God of the universe
You, who give us this wine,
Fruit of the grape and the work of men
We present to you
It will become the wine of the eternal kingdom

ANSWER : Holy God, now and always.
M Le Gall
Priest of Péderneg

Pour ce repas,
  Pour toute joie,
  Nous te louons, Seigneur !

For this meal,
For all joy
We praise to God

Bénissez Seigneur, la table
  Si bien paréc
  Emplissez aussi nos àmes
  Si affamées
  Et donnez à tous nos Frères
  De quoi manger

God, bless the table
So beautifully adorned
Also fill up our
So starving souls
And give Food
To all our brothers.

Jean Paul Briens
Péderneg
  near Begard.

BRETON

ARAOG AR PRED
"Ma Doué bénégit ar boued, a eomp da gemer evit delc 'chen da véva en ho servij - en hano an Tad hag ar Mab hag ar Spered Glan. "

BEFORE THE MEAL

God, bless the food we shall take
in order that we live for your service
In the name of Father, Son and Holy Ghost

GOUDÉ AR PRED
" Ma Doué ni ho trugaréka evit kement on d'euz kemeret evit delc'hen da véva en ho servij - en hano an Tad hag ar Mab hag ar Spered Glan "

AFTER THE MEAL
God, we thank you for all things we
have eaten in order that we live for your
service. In the name of Father and Son and Holy Ghost.

M'Feutren
Priest of Begard

Glädjens Herre var en gäst vid vart bord idag ! Gör var maltid till enfest efter Oitt behag !
Amen

TRANSLATION

The Lord of Joy be a guest at our table today !
Make our meal a feast to your pleasure
Amen

AFTER MEAL

För de gävor som Du,ger tackor vi Dig nu Du som hör förrän vi ber, prisad vare Du !
Amen

For the gifts that you gave me
we thank you now ! Lord who gives
before we pray Thou shall be praised
Amen

Bism elah Al Rahman Al Rahim.

In the name of God, the compassionate and the merciful.

**Barikna Ya rub, wa barik hatha Alfaham Abati
Anta huwa man jada Alatawi Habna an N'akouna
maa'ak, Alahu ma qudra tuka fee.
Malakutuka bil Massih rabina**

*Bless us, oh Lord, and bless this food,
My father you are the one who gives, allow us to be with you.
Oh God whose power lies in your Kingdom.*

Collected by Gill Winter in Jerusalem

**Gwyddom, O Dad, fod y rhif tri
weithiau'n troi'n bedwar gennyt ti.
Os deui yma at y bwrdd
nid pryd a gawn, bydd yma gwrdd**

Einion Evans
Winner National Eisteddfod Chair 1983

Awdur pur ein darpariaeth- rhoddwn ni
Yn rhwydd nawr wrogaeth
O'n dyheu yn gyson daeth
Yn hylaw roddion helaeth

Peter Thomas

GRAS CYMRAEG

I ti Arelwydd am ein porthant
Am ein iechyd am ein llwyddiant
Am ein heddwch an llawenydd
Y bo moliant yn dragywydd

THE WELSH GRACE

To Thee Lord for our food
For our health, for our success
For our peace and our happiness
Our Praise to Thee forever".

ALBANIA

In Albania there are 3 principal religions, Greek Orthodox, Roman Catholic and Islam. These Graces have been collected by Madame Ludmilla Stefani in Tirana and submitted to this anthology.

MUSLIM
BEFORE A MEAL

Bismil lahir rahmanir rhim
In the name of ALLAH, Most gracious, most merciful.

AFTER A MEAL

Elhamdu lil - lah
Praise be to ALLAH

BEFORE A MEAL

Jepna, O Zot, bekimin tënd ne e këtij ushqimi, që marrim prej bujarisë sate. Nëpër Krishtin, Zotin tonë. Amen

O Lord, bless us and our meal that we are taking thanks to your greatness,through Jesus our God Amen

AFTER A MEAL

Po të falemi nderës, O Zot i gjithëpushtetshëm e i amëshuar, për të gjitha bamirësitë e tua. Që jeton e sundon në shekuj të shekujve. Amen

We are thanking your honour, O Lord that is almightly for all the good things you do. You live and reign through centeries. Amen

ORTHODOX
BEFORE A MEAL

Ati ynë gë jë në qiell, u shenjtëroftë emri yt, ardhtë mbretëria jote, u bëftë dëshira jote si nëqiell e mbi dhe. Bukën tonë të përditshme jepna neve sot, dhe falna fajet tona, sikundër edhe ne ua falim fajtorëve tanë dhe mos na shtjer në ngasje, por shpëtona nga i ligu. Amen.

Our father in heaven, may your name be sainted, may your reign come,may your desire come on earth and heaven as well. You give us our daily bread, forgive our wrongdoings as we do to the others, do not urge us to mistakes but deliver us from evil. Amen.

AFTER A MEAL

Të falenderojmë O Zot i gjithëmirë se na nginje me tërë të mirat. dhe Ndricona për herë që të bëjimë punë të mira (dhe) të pëlqyera pre Tje, se Ji O Zot je ndihmësi dhe ndricuesi.
Amin.

We thank you good Lord for feeding us up with all the good things,light us to do good works that you like, because you, God are our helper and lighter. Amen

ALTÚ ROIMH BHIA

Beannaigh sinn, a Dhia,
Beannaigh ár mbia agus árdeoch.
Ós tú a cheannaigh sinn go daor,
Saor sinn ó gach olc.

GRACE BEFORE MEALS

Bless us, O God,
Bless our food and drink
As you are the one who paid dearly for us,
Deliver us from every evil

ALTÚ TAR ÉIS BIA

**Moladh leis an Rí nach gann,
Moladh gach am le Dia.
Céad moladh agus buíochas
le h Íosa Críost
i dtaobh ar ithcamar agus
a n-íosfaimid den bhia.**

GRACE AFTER MEALS

Praise to God for what we have,
Praise all time with God,
A hundred praises and thanks
to Jesus Christ
for what we have eaten
and for what we will eat

Séamas Ó Donnghaile   Béal Feirste
Collected by Ann Prys Williams

Chapter 3
Latin Graces
"Bendicto Benedicator"

ORIEL COLLEGE GRACE

Benedicte Deus, qui pascis nos a iuventute nostra et praebes cibum omni carni, reple gaudio et laetitia corda nostra, ut nos, affatim quod satis est habentes, abundemus in omne opus bonum.

Per Jesum Christum Dominum Nostrum, cui Tecum et Spiritu Sancto sit omnis honos, laus et imperium in saecula saeculorum. Amen.

Translation

Blessed God, who feeds us from our youth and provides food for all flesh, fill our hearts with joy and gladness, that we, having enough to satisfy us, may abound in every good work.

Through Jesus Christ our Lord, to whom, with You and the Holy Spirit, be all honour, praise and power for all ages. Amen

THE PROVOST   ORIEL COLLEGE OXFORD
The Revd Dr E W Nicholson,

Benedic nobis Domine Deus ! atque iis donis Tuis
quae de Tua largitate sumus sumpturi per Jesum
Christum Dominum nostrum. Amen

POST PRANDIUM

Vers.	Benedictus sit Deus in donis suis;
Resp.	Et sanctus in omnibus operibus Ejus
Vers.	Adjutorium nostrum est in nomine Domini
Resp.	Qui fecit coelum et terram.
Vers.	Sit nomen Domini benedictum;
Resp.	Ex hoc nunc usque in saecula saeculorum.
	Amen.
Oratio.	Agimus Tibi gratias, omnipotens Deus,pro

Fundatore nostro Gulielmo de Wykeham,
reliquisque quorum beneficiis hic ad pietatem et
ad studia literarum alimur, rogantes ut nos,
his donis Tuis ad Nominis Tui honorem recte
utentes, ad resurrectionis Tuae gloriam
perducamur immortalem, per Jesum Christum
Dominum nostrum.   Amen.
Fac Reginam salvam Domine;
Da pacem in diebus nostris.
Et exaudi nos in die quocunque
invocamus Te.   Amen

BEFORE LUNCH

Bless us, Lord God, and bless those gifts of yours which we, through your bounty, are to eat, through Jesus Christ, our Lord.   Amen.

AFTER LUNCH

V.   *Let God be blessed in his gifts;*
R.   *And in his works be holy.*
V.   *Our help is in the name of the Lord;*
R.   *He who made heaven and earth.*
V.   *The Lord's name be blessed;*
R.   *From this time, henceforth for ever.*
Oratio. *We give you thanks, Almighty God, for our founder, William of Wykeham, and for those others, by whose benefactions we are here brought up to godliness and good learning; beseeching you that we, rightly using these your gifts for the honour of your name, may be brought to the immortal glory of your resurrection, through Jesus Christ, our Lord.*
       Amen
       The Warden New College Oxford
       Harvey McGregor,QC,DCL

ANTE CIBUM(festal)
Gratias tibi agimus, omnipotens et aeterne Deus, pro his atque omnibus beneficiis tuis. Conserves, quaesumus, Ecclesiam Catholicam, regnum Britannicum, Reginam Elizabetham, totamque progeniem regiam, desque nobis pacem in Christo aeternam.

We give thee thanks, almighty and eternal God, for these and all thy benefits. Preserve, we beseech thee, the Catholic Church, the Kingdom of Britain, Queen Elizabeth, and all the royal family, and grant us eternal peace in Christ.

EXETER COLLEGE OXFORD
Marilyn Butler (Rector)

ANTE CIBUM

Benedic nobis, Domine Deus, et his donis, quae ex liberalitate tua sumpturi sumus, per Jesum Christum Dominum nostrum.

POST CIBUM

Versicle   Benedictus sit Deus in donis suis.
Response   Sanctus et in operibus suis.

Versicle   Adjutorium nostrum in nomine Domini.
Response   Qui fecit coelum et terras.

Versicle   Sit nomen Domini benedictum.
Response   Nunc, usque et in saecula.
Dignere, Domine Deus, largiri nobis omnibus te invocantibus propter nomen tuum sanctum vitam aeternam.

Domine Deus, resurrectio et vita credentium, qui semper es
laudandus tum in viventibus, tum in defunctis, agimus tibi
gratias pro Fundatore nostro Roberto Eglesfield, caeterisque

nostris benefactoribus, quorum beneficiis hic ad pietatem et literarum studia alimur; rogantes te ut nos, his donis recte utentes in nominis tui gloriam, ad resurrectionis gloriam perpetuam perducamur, per Jesum Christum Dominum nostrum.

Deus det vivis gratiam, defunctis requiem, Ecclesiae, Reginae, regnoque nostro pacem et concordiam et nobis peccatoribus vitam aeternam.

Bless us, Lord God, and these gifts, which of thy bounty we are about to receive, through Jesus Christ our Lord.

<u>Post</u> <u>Cibum</u>

Blessed be God in his gifts
and hallowed in his works.

Our help is in the name of the Lord
who hath made heaven and earth.

May the name of the Lord be blessed
now and for evermore.

Vouchsafe, Lord God, to bestow eternal life on us all
when we call upon thee in the holiness of thy name.

Lord God, the resurrection and the life of all who believe in thee, who art always to be praised both by the living and by the dead, we give thanks for our Founder, Robert Eglesfield,
and our benefactors, by whose charity we are here nursed in godliness and learning ; and we beseech thee that, using these gifts rightly to the glory of thy name,we may be translated to the everlasting glory of the resurrection, through
Jesus Christ our Lord.

May God grant grace to the living, rest to the departed, peace and concord to the Church, the Queen and our realm and to us sinners eternal life.
The Provost
THE QUEEN'S COLLEGE OXFORD

Oculi omnium in te sperant, Domine, et
tu das escam illorum in tempore opportuno.
Aperis tu manum tuam,
et imples omne animal benedictione.

Sanctifica nos et nostra, istisque donis, quae de tua bonitate
sumus sumpturi, benedicito, per Jesum Christum Dominum

BEFORE THE MEAL

The eyes of all wait upon thee, O Lord, and thou
givest them their meat in due season. Thou openest
thine hand and fillest every living thing with
blessing

Sanctify us and what is ours, and bless these gifts
which of thy bounty we are about to receive,
through Jesus Christ our Lord

EMMANUEL COLLEGE CAMBRIDGE
With the compliments of the Master
The Right Honourable Lord St John of Fawsley

ANTE CIBUM
Nos miseri et egentes homines
pro cibo
quem ad alimoniam corporis sanctificatum
nobis es largitus,
ut eo utamur grati
tibi, Deus omnipotens, Pater caelestis,
gratias reverenter agimus;
simul obsecrantes ut cibum angelorum,
verum panem caelestem, verbum Dei aeternum,
Dominum nostrum Jesum Christum,
nobis impertiaris,
ut per carnem et sanguinem ejus
foveamur, alamur et corroboremur.

We wretched and needy men reverently give thee thanks, almighty God, heavenly Father, for the food which thou hast sanctified and bestowed for the sustenance of the body, so that we may use it thankfully; at the same time we beseech thee that thou wouldst impart to use the food of angels, the true bread of heaven, the eternal word of God, Jesus Christ our Lord, so that our mind may feed on him and that through his flesh and blood we may be nourished, sustained and strengthened.

POST CIBUM
Quandoquidem nos, Domine, donis tuis
omnipotens et misericors Deus, exsatiasti,
effice ut posthac quid per nos fieri aut secus velis
diligenter observemus,
atque illud animo sincero effectum praestemus,
per Jesum Christum Dominum nostrum.
Domine, salvam fac Raginam.

Response   Et exaudi nos in die qua invocaverimus te.
Deus, in cuius manu sunt corda regum,
qui es humilium consolator
et fidelium fortitudo
et protector omnium in te sperantium,
da Reginae nostrae Elizabethae
populoque Christiano
triumphum virtutis tuae scienter excolere,
ut per te semper reparentur ad gloriam,
per Christum Dominum nostrum.

Since, O Lord, almighty and most merciful God, thou hast
satisfied us with thy gifts,
ensure from henceforth that we may diligently regard what
thou wishest to be done or left undone by us
and cause this to be effected with sincere heart,
through Jesus Christ our Lord

O Lord, keep the Queen safe.
And hear us in the day in which we call on thee.

God, in whose hand are the hearts of Kings,
who art the consoler of the humble
and the courage of the faithful
and protector of all who hope in thee,
grant to our Queen Elizabeth
and to the Christian people
to celebrate wisely the triumph of thy goodness
so that they may be always renewed to glory
through thee,
through Jesus Christ our Lord.

The Principal and Fellows, JESUS COLLEGE, OXFORD

Largitor omnium bonrum benedicat cibum et potum servorum suorum.

May the bestower of all gifts bless the food and drink of his servants

THE PRESIDENT, MAGDALEN COLLEGE OXFORD

Ante Cibum
    Benedictus benedicat
    May the blessed one give blessing
Post Cibum
    Benedicto benedicator
    Let praise be given to the blessed one

Sir Edward Heath

Adesto nobis, Domine Deus noster: et concede ut quos Sanctae Crucis laetari facis honore, eos donis quoque salutaribus nutrias, per Dominum nostrum Jesum Christum.

Be present with us, O Lord our God : and grant that those whom thou makest to rejoice in honour of the Holy Cross thou mayest also nourish by healthgiving gifts, through Jesus Christ our Lord.

Anon

Ante cibum
Appositis et apponendis benedicat Deus, Pater et Filius et Spiritus Sanctus.

Post cibum
Benedicatur Deo, Patri et Filio et Spiritui Sancto.

May God, the Father and the Son and the Holy Spirit, bless what is before us and what is to follow.

Thanks be to God, the Father and the Son and the Holy Spirit.

The Principle and Fellows, All Souls, Oxford

THE MATHIAS GRACE

THE MUSIC FOR THIS GRACE WAS COMPOSED BY
WILLIAM MATHIAS

Gratias tibi Domine agimus
Gratias tibi Domine agimus
Prohis et beneficus omnium tutis
Per leum Christum Dominum nostrum
Per leum Christum Dominum nostrum
Per leum Christum Dominum nostrum
Amen

submitted by H Davies
ORGANIST AND MASTER OF
CHORISTERS
ST ASAPH CATHEDRAL

CHRIST CHURCH (1546)
OXFORD

ANTE CIBUM

Nos miseri homines et egeni, pro cibis quos ad corporis subsidium benigne es largitus, tibi Deus omnipotens, Pater caelestis, gratias reverenter agimus ; simul obsecrantes, ut iis sobrie, modeste atque grate utamur. Insuper petimus, ut cibum angelorum, verum panem caelestem, verbum Dei aeternum, Dominum nostrum Jesum Christum, nobis impertiaris; utque illo mens nostra pascatur, et per carnem et sanguinem ejus foveamur, alamur, et corroboremur.

We unhappy and unworthy men do give thee most reverent thanks, almighty God, our heavenly Father, for the victuals which thou hast bestowed on us for the sustenance of the body, at the same time beseeching thee that we may use them soberly, modestly and gratefully. And above all we beseech thee to impart to us the food of angels, the true bread of heaven, the eternal word of God, Jesus Christ our Lord, so that the mind of each of us may feed on him and that through his flesh and blood we may be sustained, nourished and strengthened

Dean of Christ Church OXFORD

Ante cibum

Scholar   Benedictus sit Deus in donis suis.

Respones   Et sanctus in omnibus operibus suis.

Scholar   Adjutorium nostrum in nomine Domini.

Response   Qui fecit coelum et terras.

Scholar   Sit nomem Domini benedictum

Response   Ab hoc tempore usque in saecula.

Scholar   Domine Deus, resurrectio et vita
credentium, qui semper es laudanddus
tam in viventibus quam
in defunctis, gratias tibi agimus pro
omnibus Fundatoribus caeterisque
benefactoribus nostris, quorum beneficiis
hic ad pietatem et ad studia literarum
alimur: te rogantes ut nos, hisce tuis
donis ad tuam gloriam recte utentes, una
cum iis ad vitam immortalem
perducamur, per Jesum Christum
Dominum nostrum.

Deus det vivis gratiam, defunctis
requiem: Ecclessiae, Reginae, regnoque
nostro, pacem et concordiam: et nobis
peccatoribus vitam aeternam.

GRACE IN THE COLLEGE OF THE GREAT HALL OF THE
UNIVERSITY TO BE SAID EACH DAY BEFORE DINNER.

May the Lord be blessed in his gifts
and holy in all his works.

Our help is in the name of the Lord,
who hath made heaven and earth.

May the name of the Lord be blessed
from this time forth and for evermore.

Lord God, the resurrection and the life of those
who believe, who art always to be praised both by
the living and the dead, we give thee thanks for all
our Founders and other benefactors, by whose
benefits we are here brought up in godliness and
learning: beseeching thee that, using these thy gifts

rightly to thy glory, we amy with them be brought
to life immortal, through Jesus Christ our Lord.
May God grant grace to the living and repose to the
dead: peace and concord to the Church, to the
Queen and our kingdom: and to us sinners eternal
life.

ST CATHARINE'S (1473)
CAMBRIDGE

Ante cibum
Oculi omnium aspiciunt et inspte sperant, Domine.
Tu das iis escas illorum tempore opportuno. Aperis
tu manus et imples omne animal benedictione tua.
Benedic nobis, Dom ine, et omnibus donis tuis, quae
ex larga liberalitate tua sumpturi sumus, per
Dominum nostrum Jesum Christum.
Post cibum

Benedictus sit Dominus in donis suis. Adiutorium
nostrum in nomine Domini, qui fecit coelum et
terram. Sit nomen Domini benedictum.
Agimus tibi gratias, omnipotens Deus, pro
Fundatore ceterisque benefactoribus nostris, et pro
universis beneficiis tuis, qui vivis et regnas Deus in
saecula saeculorum. Deus conservet Ecclesiam,
Reginam, principes, regnum, veritatem et pacem.

The eyes of all look toward and trust in thee, O
Lord. Thou givest them their meats in due season.
Thou openest thine hands and fillest all living things
with thy blessing. Bless us, O Lord, and all thy gifts,
which of thy great bounty we are about to receive,
through our Lord Jesus Christ.
May the Lord be blessed in his gifts. Our help is in
the name of the Lord, who made heaven and earth.
May the name of the Lord be blessed.
We give thanks, Almighty God, for our Founder
and other benefactors, and for all thy benefits, who
livest and reignest, God for ever and ever.
May God guard the Church, the Queen, the
princes, the Kingdom, truth and peace.

Hugh Davies

CHAPTER 4

Graces from the Children of St Asaph

"Thank you for the food we eat
Thank you God for this lovely treat,
Thank you for the clothes we wear,
I hope you like this little prayer."

The following are a small selection of Graces composed by the scholars of the V.P.School,Ysgol Esgob Morgan, and St Winefreds School, all of St Asaph.

Dear God, my dog is so greedy and he jumps on the table, all homeless dogs have no food, please give them food Amen.

Rebecca Jones aged 7

Dear God, please give the poor mums and dads and children in Bosnia food, they have no food. I want them to live with fruit, vegetables and good food and live a good life and not to be too greedy and have sun and rain and thank you for my food too. Amen

Christopher Owen aged 7

Dear God, try to make my girlfriend to love me and please try to stop me from eating too much. Amen

Darin Evans aged 6

Dear God, Thank you very much for all the food I have a got, I really like it thanks a lot Amen

Anthony Bellis aged 7

Thank you God, for food and help us to share to other countries. Amen

Mathew Andrews aged 7

Dear God, I like the sunset and the sunrise because, I like the different colours and the food we eat is delicious.

Mathew Percival aged 7

Thank you for the fruit and the sweets chocolate and the fish and chips Amen

Dean Hogg aged 7

Thank you Lord for all the food we eat and try to stop me being greedy.

Justin Kelly aged 7

Dear Lord, Please help them people who haven't got food or drink. You gave us food and drink why not them, you love them just as much as us. Amen

Nicola Owen aged 10

Dear Lord, Let us think ourselves lucky for having food and drink, because some countries don't have either. We are very lucky please make us be grateful. Amen.

Jemma Bailey aged 10

Thank you for the food we eat
Thank you God for this lovely treat
Thank you for the clothes we wear
I hope you like this little prayer
Amen

Nadia Gilmartin

Thank you Jesus for our food our friends and family, I hope we'll get more food tomorrow. Amen.

Peter Bloomfield

Dear God, Thank you for all food. Thank you for the people who bring us our food on ships. Thank you for our Mums and Dads for cooking and sharing the food with us. Amen

Maria Tobin Year 3

Dear Lord, Thank you for our food if we didn't have food we would die. We need food each day to give us muscles and energy. Thank you Lord for our food and drink. Amen.

Thomas Parry aged 10

Dear Lord, Help me to see how you are good to me. Let me see how your love shows. Amen

Cheryl Roberts Year 3

Diolch i Ti am y byd
Diolch am y bwyd bob pryd
Diolch am yr haul a glaw
Diolch Dduw am popeth ddaw. Amen

School Grace- Esgob Morgan Juniors

Bless the food that lies before us,
Bless the food we are to eat,
Grant that we may eat this meal,
Willing, merry and pure of heart. Amen

Stacey Tramaseur aged 10

Dear Lord, Thank you for the food we eat, Thank you for every thing sweet, Thank you for every thing spring and fresh, Thank you for our world. Amen.

Katie Houlston aged 10

Help us not to take our food for granted, There are some people who have not got any food. Amen

Samuel James Rutherford aged 10

Please Lord help all those people in Bosnia and Rwanda who are starving We are lucky for all the food we get thankyou Lord. Amen.

Matthew Wood aged 10

Thank you for the food we eat. Thank you for carrots and meat, Thank you for every thing you have given to me. Amen.

Charlene Roberts

Thank you God for the things that we have and all the food and drink. Thank you God for our Mums and Dads and all the good things. Thank you for everything. Amen.

Michael Holmes

Jesus thank you for our friends, Thank you for all the hands we use to do everything, Thank you Jesus. Amen.

Michael Holmes

We thank you for the food,
We have just eaten,
We thank you for the school
dinners and all our meals
We pray that people in war stricken countries
May get the food they need. Amen.

Damien Davies

Thank you for are wonderful food which w'ere
going to eat. The cooks who give up their time
for us. Amen.

Thankyou for all the food we have eaten and
the drink we have drunk, Thankyou Lord for
all the food. Amen.

Sarah Jean Leach

Lord Jesus Christ, We thank you for everything. For the food you have given us. For the drink you have given to us, And for the friends that we play with. Amen

Thank you for the food you have given us thankyou for the hands that made the food, Thankyou for our families. Amen

Peter S

Dear God, Help us to understand that food is not given   to us by magic. With your help many people from all over the world provide us with food.Thank you. Amen

Zara Nicholas
Year 3

God thankyou for the food and the drinks we drink, We thank the people who have made it and we love the food we eat. Amen.

God we are all going for lunch. Bless the food we are going to eat today. Bless the hungry people and give them food. Amen.

Jodi Fishwick

For what we are about to receive may the Lord make us truly thankful. Amen.

School Grace Esgob Morgan Juniors.

Chapter 5

The Evolution Of Graces

"The Borde Is Leyd, The Clothe Spred, Now Be Grace Seyd"

In This Chapter Are Examples Of Graces As They Have
Evolved Through The Ages Taking Account Of The
Changing Circumstances Of The Time.

THE FIRST RECORDED GRACE FROM A BRITISH
SOURCE IS AN EXAMPLE OF THE PRAYERS THAT
ASKED SIMPLY FOR A BLESSING ON THE FOOD - IN
THIS CASE FOR A SPECIAL PURPOSE . IT IS *THE
BLESSING OF THE BREAD FOR A SICK PERSON,* FROM
THE PONTIFICAL OF EGBERT, ARCHBISHOP OF YORK
FROM AD 732-766

God, who recallest the wandering and savest
the penitent, affording strength to the weak and a
crown of glory to those who persevere in good
works, who by means of five loaves and two fishes
didst satisfy five thousand men who trusted in thy
mercy, be pleased to bless and hallow this bread,
that whoever shall partake thereof shall receive
health of body and protection of mind, through
Thee, Jesus Christ

THE YORK-BORN SCHOLAR ALCUIN, A MONK
OF CANTERBURY AND LATER ABBOT OF TOURS IN
FRANCE, AND HELPER OF CHARLEMANGE IN HIS
EDUCATIONAL REFORMS, WROTE A NUMBER OF LATIN
VERSES FOR INSCRIPTION IN THE DINING HALLS OF
MONASTERIES. THE FOLLOWING EXAMPLE IS IN
EFFECT A GRACE, THOUGH NOT INTENDED TO BE SAID
AS SUCH.

Bless thou, O Christ, the social feast
Here on our table spread
And every gracious gift of Thine
Upon Thy servants shed.
By Thee alone let these be blest,
Each gift Thou dost bestow,
And all are good, for They are Thine,
And Thou art good, we know.
And you, O guest, I also ask
To sing to Christ your praise,
And hymns of peace and saving grace
Unto his honour raise.

Taken from " THE YOUNG CHILDREN'S BOOK "
DATED ABOUT 1500
Before thi mete say thou thi grace,
Yt occupys bot lytell space.
'For oure mete and drynke and us
Thanke we our Lord Jhesus'.

Dr.A.Doyle
DURHAM UNIVERSITY

GEORGE BELLIN, EXETER 1565 :

God bless our meate,
God guide our waies,
God give us grace
Our Lorde to please.
Lorde longe p'serve in peace and healthe
Our gracious Queen Elizabeth. Amen.

Philip BISHOP OF WORCESTER

15th CENTURY GRACE FROM THE CITY OF LONDON
"O Thou that givest food to all flesh,
And feedest the young ravens that cry unto Thee
Fill our hearts with food and gladness
And stablish our hearts with thy grace".
In the name of the Father
And of the Son and of the Holy Ghost.

The Revd.J.R.Satterthwaite,
RETIRED BISHOP OF GIBRALTER
Also From Rt Rved. Keith Sutton
(Bishop of Lichfield)

May the blessing of the loaves & fishes
Which our Lord shared amongst the multitude
And the Grace from the King who made the
sharing Be upon us and our partaking.

Translated by The Most Revd O.Simms Archbishop of Armagh
Contributed by John & Anne Prys Williams

As my noble Father, in his wisdom,
 taught me
So may I dare to instruct you
My Lords, Ladies, Kinsmen and friends.

Serve God devoutly, and the world busily,
Do thy works wisely,
Do thine alms-giving secretly,
And answer the people demurely.

Go to thy meat appetitely
To thy supper soberly
And to thy bed-merrily

And therein, in good humour,
please thy mate duly.
Then, sleep soundly.
In the name of our precious Savour
I warrant, this physic is sound.

And so may the God we serve, sanctify
 our meat, and bless our fellowship
In the name of Christ Jesus our Lord. Amen

Rev. Frank Topping

From the 1536 PRYMER OF SALYSBERY.

Good Lord for thy Grace meekly we cal,
Blesse us and our meales and drinckys whithal ;
In nomine Patris, et Filii, et Spiritus Sancti.
(In the name of the Father and the Son and of the
Holy Ghost.)

AFTER MEAT

Blesse we Our Lord which of His Grace
Hath sent us food, good time and place ;
And blessed be the name of Our Lord
Now and ever throw all the world.
And God save our Kinge with his quene Anne
With the Catholyk Church, and send us peace
And bringe us al to His Blisse that is Endlesse,
Al Christen soulys rest in peas. Amen
('Quene Anne' is Ann Boleyn).

Pray we to God the Almighty Lorde
That sendeth fode to beastes and men
To send his blessynge on this horde,
And fede us now and ever.   Amen

THANCKES AFTER MEATE

Blessed be the Father celestiall
Who hath fed us with his material bread ;
Besechyng Hym lykewyse to fede the soule,
And graunt us his Kyngdome when we be dead.

Let all nations praise the Lord :
All peoples sing praise to God ;
Who has multiplied his mercy upon us,
And his truth endureth for ever.

QUEEN ELIZABETH the First
from a BOOK OF PRIVATE PRAYERS 1564

GEORGE BELLIN, AN IRONMONGER OF EXETER
DATED 1565

Now we have bouth meate and drinke,
Our bodies to sustayne ;
Let us remember helplesse folke,
Whom need doth cause to pine.
And like as God is merciful
To us givynge such store ;
So let us nowe be pittiful
In helping of the poor.
Then shall we find it true indeed
God will forsake us never,
But helpe us when we have most nede,
To Whome be praise for Ever. Amen

'CRUMBS OF COMFORT AND GODLY PRAYER'
(IN 1656, UNDER CROMWELL) *THE PRACTICE OF PIETY,*

O Lord bless unto our use Thy creatures at this time
provided for our sustenance, that being preserved
hereby and comforted, we may do Thee more
laudable service unto Thy glory, Who art
the author of all good , through Jesus Christ our
Lord Amen

MEMBERS OF THE KING'S PARTY AT THIS TIME COULD
DECLARE THEIR ALLEGIANCE WITH A PUNNING GRACE :

' God send this crumb well down'.

CROMWELL'S NAME WAS COMMONLY PRONOUNCED
CRUMWELL   OR CRUMMLE.

**Dust, earth, and ashes is our strength,
Our glory frail and vain ;
From earth we come, to earth at length
We shall return again.
Today we feed on flesh of beasts,
Of fowls and divers fish :
Tomorrow for crawling worms,
Our selves become a dish.
God's word doth plainly manifest
Our frailty, what it is :
Let faith and prayer be the way
To bring us unto bliss. Amen.
The whole estate of Christ His Church,
Our noble King also,
God mightily preserve and keep
From force of every foe.**

DEAN SWIFT (1667 - 1745)
AFTER DINNER WITH A MISER.

Thanks for this miracle ! This is no less
Than to eat manna in the wilderness.
Where raging hunger reigned, we've found relief,
And seen that wondrous thing, a piece of beef.
Here chimneys smoke, that never smoked before,
And we've all ate, where we shall eat no more.

SWIFT

For rabbits young and rabbits old,
For rabbits hot and rabbits cold,
For rabbits tender, rabbits tough
We thank Thee, Lord : we've had enough.

Before I take my pleasant food
I'll thank the Lord, Who is so good
In sending all I need :
Now Lord be pleased, I entreat,
To bless the food that I may eat,
And be my constant friend.

CHARLES HADDON SPURGEON 1866

We thank Thee Father, for the love
Which feeds us here below
And hope in fairer realms above
Celestial feast to know.

O Lord, who blessed the lovaes and fishes,
Look doon upon these twa bit dishes,
And though the taties be but sma' ,
Lord, make'em plenty for us a';
But if our stomachs they do fill,
'Twill be another miracle.

A nineteenth century Scottish Grace

HODGE'S GRACE

Heavenly Father, bless us,
And keep us all alive ;
There's ten of us to dinner
And not enough for five

For these, and all His other mercies, above all the crowning mercy of serious conversation, God's name be praised.

' THE BABY'S GRACE' , by R.L.GALES,

Baby's heart is lifted up
For eggs laid into the cup.
Yellow stained her praising lips
With the bread and butter strips

Aged cripples by the bed
Frugal feast on milk and bread,
And the swarthy brigand men
Eat risotto in their den.

Praise to God who giveth meat
Convenient unto all to eat :
Praise for tea and buttered toast,
Father, Son and Holy Ghost.

A COMMON GRACE

We thank Thee, Lord, for vulgar food,
For trotters, tripe, pig's cheek,
For steak and onions, with their crude
But appetising reek.

Potatoes in their jackets make
Us plain folk honour Thee;
And Thou art with us when we bake
Fresh shrimps for Sunday tea.

Thy people's praise is overdue,
But see, dear Lord, we kneel
To offer thanks for Irish stew
And tasty, cheap cowheel.

Now wait a minute, Lord ! Don't miss
The last word on our lips :
We thank Thee most of all for this,
Thy gift of fish-and-chips.

A BENISON ON WARTIME HIGH TEA

Upon this scanty meal, O Lord,
Bestow a blessing in accord :
Pour Thy grace in measure small,
Lest it more than cover all.

Bless the tiny piece of ham :
Bless the lonely dab of jam :
Bless the sparsely-buttered toast,
Father, Son and Holy Ghost.

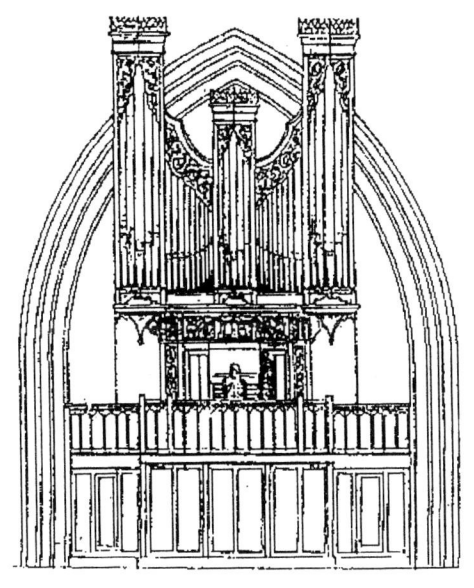

St Asaph   Cathedral
Proposed
New Organ Case

BENEDICTUS
BENEDICAT

GRACES
FOR THE
ST ASAPH CATHEDRAL

ORGAN RESTORATION APPEAL

Compiled by
DAVID T WYKE

Copyright   David T Wyke 1994

Published By   The Elwy Press
                     St Asaph
                     Clwyd   LL17 ORW

Printed By   Charter Press
                     Rhuddlan
                     Clwyd   LL18 SUA

Typiset By   Ray Forkings
                     Computech
                     St Asaph   LL17   OSU

I.S.B.N.   0 952 4 395 14

Contents

Foreword by The Very Reverend Kerry Goulstone
Dean of St Asaph

Preface   David T Wyke

The Cathedral Organ
         Hugh Davies
         Organist and Master of Choristers
         St Asaph Cathedral

Chapter 1   A Miscellany of Graces

Chapter 2   Graces in Many Languages

Chapter 3   Latin Graces

Chapter 4   Graces from the Children of St Asaph

Chapter 5   The Evolution of Graces

TO E.M.